BLOOD BROTHERS

Discover the revealing story of what
our walk with God is meant to be

SAM MASON

All Scripture quotations, unless otherwise indicated, are taken from the New International Version (NIV) of the Holy Bible, copyright 1973, 1978, 1984 by the International Bible Society. Used by permission of Zondervan. All rights reserved.

Inspiring Voices books may be ordered through booksellers or by contacting:

Inspiring Voices
1663 Liberty Drive
Bloomington, IN 47403
www.inspiringvoices.com
1-(866) 697-5313

Because of the dynamic nature of the Internet, any web addresses or links contained in this book may have changed since publication and may no longer be valid. The views expressed in this work are solely those of the author and do not necessarily reflect the views of the publisher, and the publisher hereby disclaims any responsibility for them.

Any people depicted in stock imagery provided by Thinkstock are models, and such images are being used for illustrative purposes only.

Certain stock imagery © Thinkstock.

ISBN: 978-1-4624-0661-6 (sc)
ISBN: 978-1-4624-0660-9 (e)

Library of Congress Control Number: 2013909969

Printed in the United States of America.

Inspiring Voices rev. date: 06/18/2013

CONTENTS

APPRECIATION

No man is an island. I am no exception to that axiom. My life has been greatly influenced by many godly people the Lord has brought into my life over the years. It began with my parents: James and Kathryn Mason. They reared me in the ways of God, setting a wonderful example for me with their lives of integrity and their love of the Lord and His Word. From there the list goes on without names: other family members, friends, pastors, evangelists, Sunday School teachers, singers and songwriters, inspired authors, and so many more. I believe God linked me up with all these precious folks for my benefit and His glory. To Him and them I owe a debt of gratitude. I hope that I, in turn, have been, and will continue to be, a godly influence in the lives of others . . . perhaps even you.

In particular, I wish to thank a team of family and friends who helped me make this a better book than I could have produced strictly on my own. Each of them brought their unique gifts and perspective to bear on this work. They proof-read and critiqued an earlier draft, calling my attention to typos, suggesting ways to make the message clearer at points, word it better, etc. They also encouraged me in my efforts to bring these Bible truths to you, the reader. Thanks to my dear wife and companion in life, Carol; my friend and pastor, Dr. Darrell Waller; and my friend and fellow writer, Linda Jary. Your willingness to share your time and talents is much appreciated. May God bless you for your kindness!

INTRODUCTION

Relationship . . . it's the essence of life as God intended it. Without relationship life loses it's meaning. If you're truly alone you're not really living, you're just existing. *Lonely* is in many ways a synonym for *lifeless*.

Re-examine briefly with me the account of the creation of mankind in the opening chapters of Genesis. The first mention of human beings emerges from the lips of a Maker Who is Himself a relationship. "Let *us* make man in *our* own image, in *our* likeness . . ." (Genesis 1:26). As men and women we were originally imprinted with the image of God the Father, Son, and Holy Spirit. We derived our likeness from a Creator Who has always been and always will be in relationship.

So from the very beginning man was in relationship, foremost with His Maker. We'll talk more about that in a moment. But first let's make a 360 degree visual scan of the environment into which God introduced humanity.

Returning to Genesis 1:26 we continue to read: ". . . and let them rule over the fish of the sea and the birds of the air, over the livestock, over all the earth, and over all the creatures that move along the ground." Humanity was to be related to all the animals. People were to rule over them. The concept of "rule" has gotten a bad rap because *fallen* man is inclined to be such a lousy, selfish ruler. From the Lord's perspective, however, rulership is intended to be a beneficial relationship that brings love, provision, and order to all who come under it.

Even the plants in man's surroundings were to be in a mutually beneficial relationship with human beings. These green life forms were ". . . pleasing to the eye and good for food" (Genesis 2:9), and as such were a blessing to people. In turn, "The Lord God took the man and put him in the Garden of Eden to work it and take care of it" (Genesis 2:15) so that mankind would be a blessing to the plants.

The circle of relationships for man, however, was not yet complete. Genesis 2:18 informs us that God declared: "It is not good for man to be alone. I will make a helper suitable for him." The following verses tell of the ostensible search for a helper among the animals. That exploration rendered no suitable companion, and thankfully, the Lord made man's *better half*, the woman! Thus began the marriage bond, and from that flowed family relationships and other inter-personal associations among humans.

Unfortunately, Satan and sin entered the scene through Adam's and Eve's disobedience, and all these divinely ordained relationships became flawed. Saddest of all was the perversion of the most essential of intimate bonds: that between God and mankind. This connection was to have been the source of life's greatest joys. Tragically, we read how the God/man relationship of love and trust descended into one of guilt and fear as a result of sin. "Then the man and his wife heard the sound of the Lord God as he was walking in the garden in the cool of the day, and they hid from the Lord God among the trees of the garden." (Genesis 3:8).

Now, the opening chapters of Genesis only lay the foundation for relationships as the primary theme of the Bible. The concept continues to build book by book, chapter by chapter. From cover to cover relationships dominate the discussions, and the dominate relationship discussed is the one between the Lord and the creatures originally made in His image and likeness. The last two words of Scripture before the final amen are "God's people" (Revelation 22:21). That phrase, my friend, represents the focal point of His Word to mankind.

This book I've written is about the restoration of that most precious of relationships, the one between us and our Creator. The proper function of this incredibly fulfilling connection is illustrated in the Bible through the bond enveloping two men of royal blood named David and Jonathan. Their unlikely friendship teaches us indispensable truths about what our life with God should be like.

The means through which we learn these lessons is a Bible principle we call *typology*. So just what is typology? Typology is the understanding that certain people, places, events, and things in Scripture often represent other people, places, events, and things as well. Such types may point to a future fulfillment and thus be prophetic in nature, or they may be timeless models of some general truths from God's Word.

Thus, simple types become symbols of deeper matters. Bible stories involving these types can be allegories of a sort, where the characters and happenings are representative of larger issues. That's not to suggest that types are merely poetic or fictional figures intended *only* to communicate moral teachings. In most cases they're factual historical accounts which *additionally* represent other realities.

In the chapters that follow in this book, you'll need to recognize the symbolism of key characters in the tale of two blood brothers named David and Jonathan. Understanding these types is fundamental to grasping the truths communicated by their very real story. You already know the names of the first two key characters. The third is Saul. In the fascinating narrative we're about to explore together, each one represents a person or category of people.

In order of their appearance here's what each one corresponds to . . . *Saul* is the epitome of the *carnal Christian* who trusts the Savior for their personal salvation, but never fully surrenders to Him as Lord of their lives. Saul's noble son, *Jonathan*, on the other hand, pictures the committed *spiritual believer* who not only trusts Christ for his own redemption, but seeks to yield to His will in all things. Finally, *David* in this story is a type of *Christ Himself:* Shepherd, Savior, and King.

Before we delve deeply into the principles to be learned from the lives of these three primary characters, we'll recount the backdrop that establishes the foundation for our story. The first chapter clearly sets the stage for the successive entrances of Saul, Jonathan, and David into our Biblical drama. Join me, if you will, on a journey of discovery as we observe the remarkable story of **Blood Brothers.**

CHAPTER 1

The End of an Era

He was the last and best of his kind, a righteous leader who had faithfully served Yaweh and his people virtually his whole life. He'd cast an imposing shadow over the final years of a period during which God had raised up a succession of unique leaders to guide the fledgling nation of Israel. They were called *judges*.

The root word for "judge" in this application is the Hebrew "sapat" or "shaphath." It means to judge (as between two parties at odds with one another), deliver, or rule. The responsibilities of this position were to teach the Law of the Lord, administer justice, and deliver God's people from their enemies. Roughly a dozen men and one woman served in this capacity over approximately three centuries of Jewish history. Samuel was the final leader in this era.

Yet Samuel was more than just a judge. He was prophet and priest, too. As prophet he represented God to his people. As priest he represented those same people before God. His calling to these ministries was an undeniable fact, and the love and integrity that energized his service over the years were unquestionable.

His tenure had been long and fruitful. Now Samuel was an old man and the tribal heads of Israel had gathered to ask him to step down. Amidst the intense emotion of the moment perhaps he remembered the remarkable story of his birth as passed down to him. His mother, Hannah, had been greatly loved by Samuel's father, Elkanah, but she had been unable to bear him any children. The heartache over her barrenness drove her to the Lord in desperation. She fasted, wept, and prayed for God to open her womb. The Lord heard and answered that plea.

When the firstborn of her six children arrived, she named him Samuel, meaning "God hears." His very name was a testimony to answered prayer. Yet Hannah's honoring of God through her special son was not limited to how she named him. After he was weaned, she brought him to Eli, the priest, who had overheard her original passionate request from God. She returned young Samuel to the same Tabernacle of the Lord where she had asked Yaweh for a son and vowed to subsequently give that son back to Him.

The prophet's mother was a woman of her word. Painful as it may have been, she kept her vow. "I prayed for this child, and the Lord has granted me what I asked of him. So now I give him to the Lord. For his whole life he will be given over to the Lord" (I Samuel 1:27,28). She went on to pray an eloquent prayer of rejoicing in the goodness and power of God. Then she left Samuel in the guardianship of Eli. Such was the sacred personal history others had told him about.

Samuel had vivid memories of his own to recall as he looked back over his decades of ministry. In those early years he missed his dear mother, but every twelve months she made him a new robe and took it to him during her precious visits at the time of the annual sacrifice. Meanwhile, he was growing up in the Presence of the Almighty. He even slept in the Tabernacle where the Ark of God's Presence rested. Under the tutelage of the priest he was learning to minister before God.

One night in particular had been burned indelibly into his memory. He was still just a boy at the time, perhaps around the age of twelve. He was awakened by someone calling his name. Instinctively he ran to the place where the aging, nearly blind Eli slept. The priest denied calling Samuel and told him to go back to bed. Again he heard someone call "Samuel!" Once more he went to Eli, and as before he was told to go back to sleep. A third time Samuel heard his name and again sought out his mentor. This time the old priest realized it had to be the Lord speaking. He instructed the boy to lie down, and if he heard his name yet another time, to respond: "Speak, Yaweh, for your servant is listening."

Samuel's high mileage heart managed to generate enough youthful energy to leap within him for a second or two as he remembered this, his transformational moment. Hearing a fresh word from God had been a rare thing in those days, and until that night of divine destiny the young prophet-in-training had only been told about these types of revelations. Now they began to become part and parcel of his ministry. From that day forward Samuel became the ears of Israel and the mouth of the Lord. The boy given over to Yaweh by a godly mother had gone from head knowledge *about* God to a heart relationship *with* Him.

Many years passed and Israel's premiere judge had served in holiness unto the Lord for a lifetime. Now, in the twilight of the allotted span that limits every man's earthly calling, he faced a retirement of sorts . . . what might even be considered a forced retirement at that. The elders of Israel had gathered at Samuel's home and ministry headquarters in Ramah and demanded he appoint a king to lead them! This turn of national events severely troubled the man of God. The initial sting of rejection may well have ignited personal hurt and anger. He had ruled justly and had directed Israel's ongoing victories over their powerful enemy, the Philistines. Where was the recognition of his successful efforts to fulfill his calling with diligence and integrity?

Still, Samuel pondered the situation for a moment. Perhaps his ministry was now in decline, and "yes" the elders were right, his sons did not walk in his ways. Neither of them would make a worthy successor. Maybe it was time for a change of leadership after all.

But a king? They had asked for a king to lead them so they could be like "all the other nations." At a minimum, their motivation seemed questionable. One of Samuel's earlier predecessors, Gideon, had been urged by the Jews to establish himself and his progeny as a ruling dynasty in Israel and he'd flatly refused. "The *Lord* will rule over you," he insisted (Judges 8:23). Samuel understood Gideon's concerns about the nation's inclination to conform to the pagan cultures around them. No doubt about it, Samuel was much displeased over this insistence upon having a king!

Spiritual seasoning, though, had taught the great prophet not to act on emotion alone. As was his habit when something disturbed his soul, Samuel immediately went to God in prayer. The Lord commanded His loyal servant to grant the elders their wish, then hastened to make it plain that this was not approval, but an indulgence. The divine explanation that followed is crucial to grasping the inbred tendencies not only of God's ancient chosen nation, but of every person born of Adam's race!

The final link in a centuries-long procession of Israel's judges may have taken this affront personally, but Samuel was not the one who had been the primary target of this demand for a change at the top. The Lord went on to enlighten him: ". . . It is not you they have rejected, but they have rejected me as their king. As they have done from the day I brought them up out of Egypt until this day, forsaking me and serving other gods, so they are doing to you" (I Samuel 8:7,8). Samuel's rejection was not simply a result of his age and his sons' shortcomings, it was by and large because of Who he represented: the Sovereign of the Universe Himself!

God is not against human leaders. From the beginning He's invested authority to lead in certain individuals, including Samuel. But I'm convinced that He's opposed to the absolute power that has been traditionally endowed upon human sovereigns. Kingship is a level of authority that the Lord reserves for Himself alone. No other entity in the universe has what it takes. Only the Creator has the infinite wisdom and incorruptible love necessary to rule over all with perfect justice.

God's willingness to grant Israel their wish for a king was not part of His plan to bless His children. It was a concession to the hardness of their hearts! The allowance of divorce in the law of Moses is another such example. In Matthew 19:8 Jesus said: "Moses permitted you to divorce your wives because your hearts were hard. But it was not this way from the beginning."

Yaweh gave permission for *His people to own a king* . . . or was it the other way around? Maybe He was giving permission for *a king to own His people.* Though it was not His will or plan for Israel, God had known from the outset that they would ultimately turn in that direction. In Deuteronomy 17:14-20 He had even established laws regarding the choosing and functioning of that future sovereign. The Almighty would give them what they wanted, but not without a solemn warning of the consequences. Samuel recited all the words of the Lord on this matter to the elders.

Here in essence is what they were cautioned by God: This king will conscript your sons and daughters into his service and make them serve in whatever capacity he sees fit. He'll take your fields, vineyards, and orchards to give to his officials. Your ruler of choice will then take a tenth of the flocks and harvest of the land that remains in your possession. He'll skim the cream of your servants and animals from the top to wait on him, and leave you with second best. In the final analysis you'll become his slaves! And when you at last recognize your folly and cry out to me in distress you'll be so far from me that you won't even qualify for an answer!

But their minds were made up and their ears were plugged. ". . . The people refused to listen to Samuel" (I Samuel 8:19). They were determined to follow the way of the world rather than the way of the Lord. From their conception as a nation God had wanted them to be a "kingdom of priests" (Exodus19:6) who sought and served the Lord as individuals, not needing any king but Him.

But they had chosen back then in the wilderness to stay at a distance from God and have someone else listen to Him for them, then report back. Now they wanted a king ". . . to fight our battles" (I Samuel 8:20).

The purpose of this book is to help us understand better how *our relationship with the Lord* is meant to work. But as an aside, let me point out that there is an application of the lessons of this pivotal moment in Israel's history to *the rule of human government* as well. When a people stray from God, they often end up surrendering their personal liberty to a powerful leader or government. They become willing to give up God-ordained rights and responsibilities, for the promise of security. Could the 38th president of the United States have been thinking of I Samuel 8:11-18 when he advised: "A government big enough to give you everything you want is a government big enough to take from you everything you have."?

Now, back to the issue at hand: our personal walk with the Lord. What lesson about that can we draw from the Jews' demand for a human king? As with our introduction, we need to return to Genesis to fully comprehend the implications of their decision. The insurrection at Ramah was not the first and only time Yaweh's sovereignty had been challenged. The seeds of this and every rejection of the Creator's rule, and each subsequent loss of the rich benefits of a right relationship with Him, were planted in the Garden of Eden.

God had invested massive authority in the alpha models of the human race. Every other creature on the planet was subject to their rule. Such authority, however, could only properly operate *under* that of a wise and loving Creator. It drew its legitimacy from their right relationship with Him. In the beginning that right relationship included one simple restriction: don't ever eat the fruit from the Tree of the Knowledge of Good and Evil.

Unfortunately, when temptation entered Paradise through the Devil appearing in the guise of a snake, the conspiracy that would topple this prince and princess from their thrones commenced. Satan's lies and false promises would engender a dissatisfaction with the benefits which were already theirs, and a lust for more power than was lawfully endowed. The end result of this evil craving was the loss of the divine favor Adam and Eve had enjoyed, and the initiation of a fallen nature in them . . . a nature under the authority of another god: the Devil! In essence, mankind had exchanged *blessings* in the service of the Lord for *blight* under slavery to Satan, all because they were no longer content to live under God's authority.

That fallen nature, also variously described in Scripture and by Bible teachers with such words and phrases as the "carnal man," the "carnal nature," the "old man," the "old nature," the "old self" the "sin (or sinful) nature," and the "flesh," is now the essential temperament with which every person in the world is born. It rejects the authority of God and seeks to gratify itself.

Even apparent acts of generosity and kindness toward others often have their hidden roots in selfishness. What seems altruistic may have been offered in anticipation of something in return . . . a favor from, or the approval and esteem of, others. Let's call this what it is: selfish manipulation. The Apostle Paul recognized these tendencies in himself and proclaimed his own moral bankruptcy. "I know that nothing good lives in me, that is, in my sinful nature. For I have the desire to do what is good, but I cannot carry it out" (Romans 7:18).

This carnal nature within loves to masquerade as the real us. It demands that its lawless desires become ours. We tend to automatically assume that what it wishes is what we wish, and that satisfying those wants is what will bring us true fulfillment. But understand that this *old* nature is a perversion of the original character of the wholesome creatures we were made to be. The Lord now wants to give us a *new* nature, which is very much like the initial one given to mankind in the Garden of Eden. That new nature is the real you, and is made for sweet and unbroken fellowship with God.

There was and is only one way to effectively deal with the dilemma of human beings created in the image of God, but now reduced in many respects to the likeness of the evil one. The solution is death, then resurrection! This way out was ultimately provided in Christ Jesus. "For we know that our old self was crucified with him so that the body of sin might be done away with, that we should no longer be slaves to sin" (Romans 6:6). "In the same way, count yourselves dead to sin but alive to God in Christ Jesus" (Romans 6:11).

The Bible story we're prayerfully examining in this book is a valuable illustration of the aforementioned dilemma and its solution. So let's continue our pursuit of the truths to be uncovered as we follow along with the children of Israel as they enter a new era. This account can help us better understand how to walk in sweet fellowship with our Maker. And deep within the heart of each of us, isn't that what we sincerely desire?

CHAPTER 2

Try This on for Size

In his prime at thirty years of age he was an impressive physical specimen, with the potential to be an impressive leader as well. He was the son of a man of standing in Israel, his father possessing wealth, strength, and courage. He himself was as handsome as they come, and stood a head taller than his fellowmen. This chosen man from the tribe of Benjamin would soon ascend to the throne and rule over God's people. Would he be a good fit for that throne? He would don a crown that would carry great authority and require great wisdom. Would the crown be a good fit for him?

Time and the tide of events would reveal the answers to these questions. For now, this man named Saul was content to be carrying out a simple domestic errand. His father, Kish, had been missing some donkeys and sent his son and one of the household servants on a search and recovery mission. They covered a lot of ground but found no trace of the lost animals. By this time Saul suspected his dad would stop worrying about the missing donkeys and start worrying about his son and his servant instead.

This unsuspecting king-in-waiting would have turned back for home, but the servant had another suggestion. He noted that there was a highly respected man of God in a nearby town, who was widely known to hear from the Lord. In fact, his ability was so reliable that everything this prophet said came true. "Let's go there now. Perhaps he will tell us what way to take" (I Samuel 9:6), suggested the servant.

Saul was hesitant at first, thinking they should have something to give this exceptional man in return for his help. Realizing that he and his servant had exhausted their limited provisions, he assumed they had nothing left to offer the prophet of God. But the servant declared he had a quarter of a shekel of silver in his possession, so the proposed side trip was on. Unbeknownst to the wandering pair, this spur-of-the-moment suggestion would lead to a divine encounter.

As they approached their destination, Saul and his companion came across some girls headed out to draw water. When they inquired about the location of the prophet, the two of them got their first hint that the Lord's favor was very much upon this thing. The girls indicated that the men's timing was remarkably fortunate. The man of God had just arrived that day for a sacrifice at the high place dedicated to the worship of Yaweh, with a feast to follow. "Go up now," they advised, "you should find him about this time" (I Samuel 9:13).

Only the day before, God had tipped off the prophet to the soon arrival of a special man from the land of Benjamin. Samuel was to anoint him as the first King of Israel. This new leader would then deliver his people from the oppression of the cruel Philistines.

Samuel didn't have to wait long. Just twenty-fours after he had heard from the Lord, his faith became sight as he caught a glimpse of Saul, and Yaweh confirmed: "This is the man I spoke to you about. He will govern my people" (I Samuel 9:17). Samuel now knew who Saul was. Saul, however, had no idea who Samuel was, and a moment later asked him for directions to the prophet's house. The man of God identified himself to the one soon to be crowned king, then downloaded a heap of unanticipated divine data that surely dazed its recipient.

Saul would find the next few minutes stunning, the subsequent hours life-changing, and the following week a period of somewhat bewildering contemplation. It appeared that the prophet had been expecting him. A seat of honor with a previously set aside choice cut of meat awaited him at the sacrificial feast that day. Saul would stay the night, then Samuel would ultimately tell him everything that God had to say to him before letting him go in the morning.

The final piece of information to come Saul's way in their initial encounter was in the form of a rhetorical question from Samuel. "And to whom is the desire of Israel turned, if not to you and all your father's family?" (I Samuel 9:20). Saul probably gathered that some kind of special honor and/or responsibility was inferred, but I can almost read his puzzled thoughts in that instant . . . "What's *that* all about?"

When he spoke, Saul's response seemed to reflect true humility. "But am I not a Benjamite, from the smallest tribe of Israel, and is not my clan the least of all the clans of the tribe of Benjamin? Why do you say such a thing to

13

me?" (I Samuel 9:21). That same humble spirit would be evident again in another week.

Saul dined with Samuel and about thirty other guests that day. The prophet talked again with Saul after the feast, though the content of that chat is not recorded in Scripture. In any event, the most momentous conversation yet between the two was just around the corner. Did the son of Kish sleep a wink at Samuel's house that night? I wonder . . .

They arose at sunrise and Samuel sent Saul on his way, accompanying him on the journey for a short while. As they headed to the edge of town, he stopped and instructed Saul to command the servant to go on ahead so the pair could be alone. The man of God had a message from God. The shy guy from the little tribe of Benjamin was about to experience some potent course altering events.

Samuel took out a container of oil, poured it on Saul's head and kissed him. The freshly anointed candidate then heard these astounding words flow from the lips of Samuel: "Has not the Lord anointed you leader over his inheritance?" (I Samuel 10:1). Of all the men in the fledgling nation, Saul had been chosen to be their first ever king! Oil in the Bible is typical of the Holy Spirit, so we understand that the emptying of the flask of oil over Saul's head was more than just an attempt to groom his hair. It represented his anointing for service by the Spirit of God Himself.

It's important here to observe that although Israel had requested and were given a king, Saul was not anointed as such. Yes, they had asked for a *king* [Hebrew—"melek"] (I Samuel 8:5), but Saul's anointing was only as a *leader*

[Hebrew—"nagid"] (I Samuel 10:1). God had allowed them to fulfill their carnal desire for a king, but He would not empower this man with the absolute sovereignty reserved for the Lord alone!

There followed a citation by Samuel of three imminent events that would confirm Saul's high calling and prepare him for it. The first would demonstrate Yaweh's ability to deal with the newly appointed leader's domestic issues: the recovery of the lost donkeys. The second revealed the Lord's provision for Saul's physical needs: bread and wine. The third dealt with his requirement for spiritual wisdom and power to rule God's own chosen people: a divine encounter. I encourage you to read the details in I Samuel 10:2-7.

These events and their foretelling remind us that the Lord never bestows a calling on His child without providing a means to carry it out. If you fully commit your ways to Him, He'll watch over your family and household affairs. He'll meet your physical and material needs. Finally, God will provide the spiritual associations, skills, and strength necessary to fulfill your divine mission.

Before they parted, Samuel told Saul that he would later join him in Gilgal to sacrifice offerings to the Lord. He warned him to be patient during this week of waiting. Then another amazing thing happened: God changed Saul's heart on the spot! What does that mean? I believe this Old Testament experience was equivalent to the New Testament experience of being "born again" (see John 3:3-8). Hadn't Samuel advised Saul: ". . . you will be changed into a different person" (I Samuel 10:6)?

No one can be an effective leader of God's people without a vibrant personal relationship with the Lord. And that vibrant personal *relationship* begins with a personal *faith* which results in a changed heart. I'm convinced that Saul took the Word of the Lord through the lips of Samuel by faith. That act of faith brought about a remarkable transformation on the inside of Israel's king-elect.

Peter described that kind of change in Acts 15:9 where he declared that Gentiles as well as Jews had now been born again. "He (God) made no distinction between us and them, for he purified their hearts by faith." Paul later further defined this experience in II Corinthians 5:17: "Therefore if anyone is in Christ, he is a new creation; the old has gone, the new has come!" This internal transformation of Saul was the most essential aspect of his preparation for a life of godly leadership.

After the fulfillment of Samuel's prophecies of the three confirmational events, the last of which found Saul himself prophesying amidst a procession of prophets, Saul headed for the local high place. He may have gone there simply to worship and thank God for the calling and gifts he had received. I suspect, though, that his motive was additionally, if not primarily, to seek the Lord's help in sorting out this whirlwind of information and proceedings that had likely left his head spinning.

Whether Saul subsequently ran into his uncle at that high place, or at home after his own arrival there, we're not told. But in response to his relative's query: "Where have you been?", he revealed that he'd been searching for his father's donkeys, and being unable to locate them, had sought help from Samuel. Asked what the prophet had said, Saul only recounted Samuel's assurance that the donkeys had already been found. He mentioned nothing of what the man of God had told him of his becoming king. This would seem to be another indication of Saul's perplexity and/or humility.

More evidence of his state of mind arose a few days later at his coronation ceremony. Samuel summoned the children of Israel to Mizpah to meet with the Lord and discover their king. Before commencing the procedures by which this new leader would be chosen, the man of God made it clear that Yaweh had proven Himself faithful to Israel and that their demand for a king was in truth a rejection of their God (I Samuel 10:18,19).

It appears likely that a method of casting lots, used in a number of instances in Scripture to discern the will of God, was used here to confirm the Lord's choice for king. Step by step the field was narrowed. First one tribe was chosen, then a particular clan within that tribe, and finally it came down to a single man. But when Saul, son of Kish, was selected, the candidate was no where to be found. So they sought a word from the Lord, and He revealed that Saul had hidden himself among the baggage.

It was obvious that Saul had not *pursued* kingship. He had little or no confidence in himself. He was reluctant to ascend to a position of such great responsibility. For now at least, the first king of Israel was a man of humility. Unlike worldly standards, this is often the criteria God uses in choosing leadership. Moses was "a very humble man, more humble than anyone else on the face of the earth" (Numbers 12:3). Christ Himself professed ". . . I am gentle and humble in heart . . ." (Matthew 11:29).

Although some valiant men, whose hearts God had touched, quickly attached themselves to the new king, others were unimpressed, perhaps because of Saul's reticent and humble reaction to the honor bestowed upon him. "How can this fellow save us?", (I Samuel 10:27) they complained. The new king could have reacted with anger, but if he did feel any irritation he held his tongue. Even after his first military victory, when the people called for those previous cynics to be executed, Saul declared "No one shall be put to death today, for this day the Lord has rescued Israel" (I Samuel 11:13).

That initial success in battle came in the wake of an Ammonite siege of Jabesh Gilead in the region belonging to the tribe of Manassah. The men of that city tried to make peace with the warring Ammonites, but a grievous condition was placed upon their treaty request. The enemy's leader, Nahash, would only spare them if they submitted to having their right eyes gouged out. This was meant to bring disgrace not only to Jabesh Gilead, but the whole nation of Israel. The city elders requested a week to deliberate, and sent word of their dilemma to Saul.

When Saul heard the news, the Holy Spirit descended on him in power and he burned with anger. His swift and decisive action resulted in the gathering of an army of three-hundred thirty-thousand men, and his clever military strategy led to a total triumph over the Ammonites. The young ruler had shown himself to be a capable leader. Following the victory Samuel reassembled the people, this time at Gilgal, to reaffirm the kingship of Saul.

Despite the euphoria of this great celebration, the retiring leader had some sober words for the children of God. First Samuel asked them to testify if he had ever done them any wrong. If he had, he would make it right. "'You have not cheated or oppressed us,' they replied. 'You have not taken anything from anyone's hand'" (I Samuel

12:4). Samuel subsequently recounted numerous mighty acts of the Lord on Israel's behalf over the centuries.

Then came the most ominous words of Samuel's farewell address. He left no question as to their sinful motives when they demanded a king. In a demonstration of Yaweh's displeasure Samuel would send thunder and rain upon their wheat harvest . . . weather that was virtually unheard of at that time of year and would endanger the harvest. Samuel ended this indictment with a stinging rebuke. "And you will realize what an evil thing you did in the eyes of the Lord when you asked for a king" (I Samuel 12:17). The apparently penitent crowd pled for Samuel's prayers on their behalf.

Harsh truths aside, the last of Israel's judges ended his homily largely with words of compassion. "Do not be afraid" (I Samuel 12:20) was his immediate response. He encouraged the people to think about the great things the Lord had done for them, to serve Him with all their hearts, and not turn to useless idols. "For the sake of his great name the Lord will not reject his people, because the Lord was pleased to make you his own. As for me, far be it from me that I should sin against the Lord by failing to pray for you" (I Samuel 12:22,23).

Samuel's spiritual ministry would continue until the day he died. But his judicial and military leadership had come to its final conclusion. Humanly speaking, the nation's future was now in the hands of Saul. Would he be a good fit for the throne? Would the royal crown be a good fit for him?

CHAPTER 3

The Bankruptcy of the Carnal Nature

Time had passed and something "old" within Israel's first man of royalty began to rear its ugly head against the "new" Saul. It had been lurking inside him for a long time, but its first emergence in the divinely authorized account of his life is recorded in I Samuel chapter 13.

Saul's eldest son, Jonathan had provoked a massive battle by attacking the Philistine outpost at Geba. We're not told why this attack was initiated or whether or not the young prince was acting on his father's orders. But when Israel's oppressors caught wind of it, this relatively minor skirmish exploded into a major conflict. Had Saul's hand been forced by his son's action, or had he himself intended to go to battle?

In their fierce reaction, the Philistines rallied three-thousand two-man chariots, and foot soldiers "as numerous as the sand on the seashore" to their camp at Micmash. Saul's call to arms, however, elicited no such numbers of volunteer soldiers on the Israeli side. In fact, the response of Jews in the area was to flee away across the Jordan River or hide in "caves and thickets, among the rocks, and in pits and cisterns." Even the three-thousand soldiers already stationed with Saul and Jonathan "were quaking with fear."

In his concern (or was it panic?) over the already small army around him now beginning to disperse in fear, Saul felt obliged to act. Samuel had commanded him to wait seven days for his arrival, but when the aged man of God did not get there on schedule, the king decided to himself act in the role of the missing priest. Big mistake! Apparently Samuel had not been *that* late. He arrived *just* as Saul had finished the ceremonial offerings. "What have you done?" He demanded (I Samuel 13:11).

Saul's motive in offering the sacrifices is not entirely clear in the Bible's account. Was it fear, impatience, arrogance, or all of the above? His excuse was that events were getting out of hand, and he had not yet sought Yaweh's favor for the battle. In Samuel's absence the king felt compelled to carry out the duties reserved for the priest. "You have acted foolishly" was Samuel's spiritual assessment of the matter.

Whatever Saul's motives may have been, the bottom line was that he had disobeyed God's directive to await the prophet's arrival before taking any action. Samuel quickly got to the heart of the issue: "You have not kept the command the Lord your God gave you" (I Samuel 13:13).

In our walk with the Lord it usually comes down to two essential things: faith and obedience. The Apostle Paul's most fundamental epistle begins and ends with this premise. The purpose of the Gospel of Christ is to bring people ". . . to the *obedience* of *faith*" (Romans 1:5), ". . . so that all nations might *believe* and *obey* him"

(Romans 16:26). These two elements are indispensable for successful godly living. However, King Saul appears to have acted in unbelief and disobedience.

Centuries after Saul, another king would commit a similar sin. Uzziah's early successes led to pride and unfaithfulness to God. He entered the temple of the Lord to burn incense on the altar, a duty restricted by God to the priests. Such blatant disobedience ultimately led to disease and death for him. You can read the account in II Chronicles 26:16-21.

Saul's transgression also carried a penalty, though perhaps not as severe as the one dealt Uzziah. Samuel addressed Saul under the unction of the Holy Spirit. "But now your kingdom will not endure; the Lord has sought out a man after his own heart and appointed him leader of his people, because you have not kept the Lord's command" I Samuel 13:14). Having delivered the Word of the Lord to the wayward king, the prophet departed.

Granted, Saul's detachment of three-thousand had been reduced to a mere six-hundred against a Philistine army which had to have numbered at least in the six figure range. And due to an enemy ban on blacksmiths in Israel, among those several hundred Israeli soldiers only Saul and Jonathan had a sword or spear. Yet even with just a cursory knowledge of Israel's history the king should have remembered that Gideon had once defeated a huge military force with just three-hundred men, armed only with torches.

Saul may not have acted in faith, but his son was about to do just that. Unlike his father, Jonathan wasn't worried about the size of *his* detachment. He and his armor-bearer determined to take the offensive and raid a

Philistine outpost. To say the pair were badly outnumbered would be an understatement. Nevertheless, their trust in God prevailed, and together they killed some twenty of the enemy in short order. Far beyond the scope of that relatively minor opening victory, the Lord then sent a colossal panic upon the whole Philistine army . . . one that would lead to a remarkable rout!

Saul's scouts soon observed the enemy's troops in utter disarray, and reported it to their commander. A hasty reading of the account of his reaction to this turn of events may not give one the sense that anything significant was awry. But a closer look at the story is quite telling.

Saul had initially called for the ark of God and a priest in an obvious effort to seek the counsel of the Lord before engaging the enemy. As the noise from the commotion in the Philistine camp continued to intensify, however, the king cut short the priest's divine consultation. "Withdraw your hand," (I Samuel 14:19) he commanded. It seems Saul felt his own judgment was now sufficient, and waiting for a word from God unnecessary. Off to battle they went.

Their efforts to take full advantage of Yaweh's intervention on Israel's behalf, though, would be hampered by an imprudent oath uttered by their leader. "Cursed be any man who eats food before evening comes, before I have avenged myself on my enemies!" (I Samuel 14:24). This proclamation not only left the troops unable to renew their energy during an exhausting fight, it revealed Saul's self-absorption. Take note of his use of the words *I, myself,* and *my.*

Clearly the king's paramount concerns were not for the Lord or His people, but for himself! In his mind it was *Saul's* honor, *Saul's* kingdom, and *Saul's* reputation which were at stake. As it turned out, he was even willing to kill the very man whose faith and initiative had led to this wonderful victory: his son, Jonathan!

Unaware of his father's edict, the young prince had reinvigorated himself with some honey providentially discovered in the woods where the battle had ventured. Following a resounding victory over the Philistine army, the foolish king sentenced his son to death for this act (I Samuel 14:44). Had it not been for the intervention of Saul's own soldiers (I Samuel 14:45), the hero of the battle of Micmash would have been executed!

If Saul's misbehavior at this battle dashed any expectation of a family dynasty, his disobedience in the next military action would radically alter his personal standing before God. No mere human venture, the next conflict would be a divine assignment.

Samuel delivered the orders. "This is what the Lord Almighty says: 'I will punish the Amalekites for what they did to Israel when they waylaid them as they came up from Egypt. Now go, attack the Amalekites and totally destroy everything that belongs to them. Do not spare them; put to death men and women, children and infants, cattle and sheep, camels and donkeys'" (I Samuel 15:2,3). The king mustered two-hundred ten-thousand men and set out for the city of Amalek.

After allowing the pro-Israeli Kenites to flee the danger zone, the army attacked. But something was askew with Saul's strategy. "He took Agag king of the Amalekites alive, and all his people he totally destroyed with the sword. But Saul and the army spared Agag and the best of the sheep and cattle, the fat calves and lambs—everything that was good. These they were unwilling to destroy completely, but everything that was despised and weak they totally destroyed" (I Samuel 15:8,9).

The king may have been happy with the outcome of the conflict, but the Lord was not! He revealed Saul's disobedience, and His grief over it, to Samuel. The righteous justice of Yaweh had been thwarted by an insubordinate commander. The troubled prophet cried out to God in prayer all night long.

Early the next morning he sought out the king. But Saul was missing. Samuel was told that the prideful leader had gone to Carmel, set up a monument in his own honor, then headed down to Gilgal. Saul's first words upon Samuel's arrival there reflected self-deceit at best, and outright dishonesty at worst. "The Lord bless you!" he said to the prophet, "I have carried out the Lord's instructions" (I Samuel 15:13). To which the man of God responded, "What then is this bleating of sheep in my ears? What is this lowing of cattle that I hear?" (I Samuel 15:14).

At that point the spillway of Saul's reservoir of lame excuses opened wide. He blamed his failure to obey Gods' command on the soldiers, then attempted to justify it by claiming these livestock were only spared to sacrifice to the Lord. The prophet would have none of this protest. "Stop!" Samuel said to Saul. "Let me tell you what the Lord said to me last night" (I Samuel 15:16).

Samuel's opening statement following Saul's consent to listen, struck the king right between the eyes. "Although you were once small in your own eyes, did you not become the head of the tribes of Israel?" (I Samuel 15:17). A big part of Saul's drift from God was his journey from humility to self-importance. He was not in need of more *self-esteem*, he desperately required greater *God-esteem*.

Samuel went on to clearly contrast God's command and the king's lack of compliance with it.

Despite the sting of this first blow, Saul continued his stream of defensive explanations. Beginning with a huge "But" (I Samuel 15:20,21), the king complained that he *did* obey the Lord. He went on to recount how he *completely destroyed* the Amalekites, while *sparing* their king and the best of the sheep and cattle as plunder. Somehow in his twisted logic, Saul failed to recognize this as a contradiction in terms and a failure to obey God's command to spare *nothing* that belonged to the enemy! The bottom line was that like the carnal Christian, Saul attempted to create his own terms of obedience, picking and choosing the parts he liked, or with which he was willing to comply.

Samuel responded with these words: "Does the Lord delight in burnt offerings and sacrifices as much as in obeying the voice of the Lord? To obey is better than sacrifice, and to heed is better than the fat of rams. For rebellion is like the sin of divination, and arrogance like the evil of idolatry. Because you have rejected the word of the Lord, he has rejected you as king" (I Samuel 15:22,23).

Finally, Holy Spirit conviction struck home and Saul confessed that what he had done was in reality sin. He claimed that his disobedience was because he feared the people, and therefore gave in to their desires to retain the best of the plunder. He begged Samuel to come back with him, allegedly so he could worship the Lord.

Samuel initially refused and turned to go. Saul tugged at his mentor's robe in an effort to detain him. It ripped, and Samuel used this as an illustration to remind Saul that God had torn the kingdom from him to give to a better man.

The rejected king reiterated his confession of sin, but followed it up with a request which raises questions about the sincerity of his repentance in the matter. ". . . Please honor me before the elders of my people and before Israel . . ." (I Samuel 15:30). He seemed less concerned with worshipping the Lord and more concerned with regaining his personal prestige! Saul went on to expose the distance already developing between the king and his God when he referred to Yaweh as *Samuel's* God (I Samuel 15:30).

Samuel relented after a second request to accompany Saul, and he and the king worshipped Yaweh together. The prophet then carried out the death sentence on Agag, king of Amalek, that Saul had failed to act upon. "As your sword has made women childless, so will your mother be childless among women" (I Samuel 15:33) declared the prophet to the condemned man.

A fascinating epilog of sorts may be found in the book of Esther. Centuries after the sparing of King Agag by Saul, an apparent descendent of this Amalekite king (Esther 3:1) extended his ancestor's legacy of hostility against the people of God. Haman had wheedled his way into an exalted position in the court of King Xerxes of the Persian Empire. Incensed by one Jew's refusal to kneel at his feet, Haman used his manipulative influence to persuade Xerxes to sign an order to exterminate every Jew in his kingdom.

Through the faith and obedience of Queen Esther and her adoptive father, Mordecai, the plot was thwarted. To this day the Jewish people celebrate this victory as the "Feast of Purim." But the account of Haman's diabolical efforts demonstrates the relentless war between good and evil, spirit and flesh. It stands as a warning against affording even a toehold to the enemy of our souls.

Samuel left for his home in Ramah and would never again in this life see the man of the tribe of Benjamin whom he had anointed king of Israel. Soon, however, he would anoint his successor. Although Saul had shown himself to be a valiant and victorious military leader, he'd badly missed the mark in his relationship with God. In the remaining years of his reign we occasionally catch glimpses of a fading aspiration to be an honorable leader, but overall the picture that emerges is that of a man too much dominated by wrong desires.

What was it inside of Saul that brought him to this place of unbelief and rebellion? It was that evil entity we mentioned briefly in chapter 1, variously known as the "carnal man," the "carnal nature," the "old man," the "old nature," the "old self" the "sin (or sinful) nature," and the "flesh." It's origin is in the Garden of Eden where the first man and woman attempted to become their own gods, and inadvertently made Satan their god. The frightening thing is that this entity resides within every human being ever since sin entered the lives of our ancient ancestors Adam and Eve. We're *born* with it.

Those who are *born again* through faith in Christ (who is the *Last* Adam—I Corinthians 15:45) receive a *new* nature, one that is righteous rather than sinful. "For just as through the disobedience of the one man the many were made sinners, so also through the obedience of the one man the many will be made righteous" (Romans 5:19). Through Jesus the old nature was given the death sentence. "For we know that our old self was crucified with

29

him so that the body of sin might be done away with . . ." (Romans 6:6).

The death of the carnal nature is legally an accomplished fact in Christ. But that fact must be personally applied in faith by us as believers. ". . . count yourselves dead to sin but alive to God in Christ Jesus" (Romans 6:11). "Those who belong to Christ Jesus have crucified the sinful nature with its passions and desires" (Galatians 5:24). "So I say, live by the Spirit, and you will not gratify the desires of the sinful nature. For the sinful nature desires what is contrary to the Spirit, and the Spirit what is contrary to the sinful nature. They are in conflict with each other . . ." (Galatians 5:16-17). Jesus taught that the death of this old nature is not simply a one-time event, but an ongoing process. "If anyone would come after me, he must deny himself and take up his cross daily and follow me" (Luke 9:23).

God has declared that carnal nature to be *totally bankrupt*. The Apostle Paul concurred wholeheartedly. "I know that nothing good lives in me, that is, in my sinful nature" (Romans 7:18). We make a strategic mistake if we think we can salvage anything from the ways of the old man within and make it serviceable for the Kingdom of God. It's fit for nothing but the grave!

This requirement to appropriate God's victory over the old self was where Saul failed. As we noted in Chapter 2, he was given a new heart by the Lord and changed into a different person. Yet he failed to operate in the power of that Spirit-created godly being inside him. While he won many military campaigns, Saul lost the war within against the old nature.

Did he fully turn his back on God? I don't believe so. In his final days Saul seemed to genuinely acknowledge his failures. To David he admitted "Surely I have acted like a fool and have erred greatly" (I Samuel 26:21). And eventually he appeared to surrender to God's will. "Then Saul said to David, 'May you be blessed, my son David; you will do great things and surely triumph'" (I Samuel 26:25). Finally, we have the testimony of Samuel, who supernaturally appeared to the desperate king the day before he would die in battle and implied Saul's imminent arrival in Paradise. ". . . tomorrow you and your sons will be with me" (I Samuel 28:19).

Saul is typical of carnal Christians, trusting Jesus Christ as Savior, but not fully surrendering to Him as Lord and King. He's an example of believers who never live up to the high calling of God. Not only do they not experience the abundance of joy that's the product of a life completely surrendered to the Lord, but sadly, they also fail to bring that same joy to the heart of the Father.

Wilbur Rees captured much of the attitude of the carnal Christian in the following:

> I would like to buy $3 worth of God, please.
> Not enough to explode my soul or disturb my
>   sleep,
> but just enough to equal a cup of warm milk
> or a snooze in the sunshine.
> I don't want enough of God to make me love a
>   black man
> or pick beets with a migrant.
> I want ecstasy, not transformation.
> I want warmth of the womb, not a new birth.
> I want a pound of the Eternal in a paper sack.
> I would like to buy $3 worth of God, please.

Exchange the dollars for shekels, and in many ways that's probably an apt description of Saul's approach to life.

It's significant that the act that finally brought about Saul's rejection as king was his unwillingness to entirely destroy Amalek as God had commanded him. You see, Amalek is typical of the carnal nature. He was the grandson of Esau, who as the eldest son of the patriarch Isaac, sold his birthright for a pot of stew. Esau is described in Hebrews 12:16 as "godless." His descendents attacked God's chosen people in an attempt to prevent them from entering the Promised Land. In the wake of that assault, Moses declared "The Lord will be against the Amalekites from generation to generation" (Exodus 17:16).

Historically that war continued for centuries. Saul was given the mission to bring it to its conclusion' but disobeyed. Figuratively, however, the battle against Amalek continues in the lives of Christians everywhere who pursue righteousness. Amalek remains a type of the old nature. Are you, by the power of the new nature and the Spirit of the Lord within you, engaged in that battle against the flesh in your life?

Remember the opening and closing questions from Chapter 2? The answers are that Saul was not a good fit for the throne, and the crown was not a good fit for him. The fact is, that in the end the throne and crown of true kingship belong only to the King of Kings. All rightful authority in the universe must flow from His dominion alone. Any attempt to usurp His sovereignty will conclude in utter disaster. Life at its best is enjoyed in the shadow of God's throne.

C H A P T E R 4

A Noble Son

Heredity or environment . . . which wields the most influence when it comes to the development of a human being? I remember our biology teacher, Mr. Dingel, posing that question to us in high school. I know that the ensuing discussions included proponents of both sides of that issue. I don't recall whether the conclusion of the matter favored heredity or environment.

There is no question that both factors play powerful roles in who we become as individuals. The genes passed down from our parents predetermine not only physical attributes, but aspects of our personality. Family and other influential people near and far, plus personal experiences, contribute to the development of our thought processes and overall philosophy of life. But in the end the prevailing dynamic is personal choice. Our decisions largely determine who we are.

Children of good parents may become bad characters or vice versa. Our background might teach us one way of life, while we select a totally different path for ourselves.

We're not simply a product of our circumstances. God has given each of us free will, and that entails personal responsibility.

We must ultimately decide what kind of people we will become. The great leader Joshua understood this. He challenged the Israelites: ". . . if serving the Lord seems undesirable to you, then choose for yourselves this day whom you will serve . . ." (Joshua 24:15). He went on to proclaim that he and his family had chosen to serve the Lord.

Jonathan is a graphic illustration of this principle. His father, Saul, had begun well, but made bad decisions and eventually surrendered in large part to the dictates of his lower nature. Jonathan possessed much of the same genetic makeup as his father. He also had that poor example lived in front of him for many years. Yet the nobility that became Saul's in title only, would be the core of Jonathan's integrity because of the righteous decisions he made.

Like Jonathan, we too have a genetic heritage that is less than desirable. In the flesh we're descended from fallen Adam, born with an inbred penchant for selfishness and sin. In Romans 7:14,15 Paul expresses this frustrating condition clearly. ". . . I am unspiritual, sold as a slave to sin. I do not understand what I do. For what I want to do I do not do, but what I hate I do."

Righteous decisions are what make the difference in who we are and who we become . . . beginning with the decision to surrender our lives to Christ by faith. The remedy for our sinful Adamic nature is found only in Jesus. "For if, by the trespass of the one man [Adam], death reigned through that one man, how much more will those who receive God's abundant provision of grace and of the gift of righteousness reign in life through the one man, Jesus Christ" (Romans 5:17). That gift of righteousness comes only through our decision to fully trust in Jesus. Just as Jonathan had to eventually surrender in faith to David's God-given authority, so we must fully yield to the claims of Christ.

Jonathan initially appears in the sacred record in I Samuel 13:2. Originally we're only told that he commanded one-third of Saul's standing army at Gibeah in Benjamin. His age is not specified, but using information provided elsewhere in I Samuel, we can determine that he was quite young, perhaps even in his teens. That he was appointed to such a responsible position as a youth says much about the level of confidence his father had in him. His sterling character is noticeably implied by the context surrounding the very first mention of his name.

The next verse reports what is probably his inaugural military action at Gebah. We talked about this briefly in the last chapter, wondering whether Jonathan was acting on his father's command, or on his own initiative, in attacking the Philistine outpost. Although the narrative doesn't answer that question directly, based on other factors I'm inclined to draw my own conclusion.

King Saul's announcement to the Hebrew nation might lead one to believe that he himself had given the order for Jonathan to attack. "*Saul* has attacked the Philistine outpost, and now Israel has become a stench to the Philistines" (I Samuel 13:4). Yet I think this wording was a product of the king's ego (carnal nature) attempting to take credit for the courageous effort of his son. Given what we read of Jonathan later, I believe it was his faith in the Lord, rather than his father's command, that led him to take the offensive against the enemy of God's people.

The fearful prospect of Saul's already small army diminishing to nothing, led the king to disobey the Lord, usurp Samuel's priestly office and present the burnt offering himself. While Saul was acting in the flesh, Jonathan was acting in the Spirit. Instead of being troubled by the small number of Israel's soldiers, Jonathan set out on a venture of faith.

Unlike his previous assault on the enemy outpost at Geba, there's no question about who took the initiative in Jonathan's next skirmish with the enemy. He was not ordered by his father, and in fact did not even tell his father about it, according to Scripture (I Samuel 14:1). Jonathan and his armor-bearer headed out on their own for the Philistine outpost on the other side of the pass at Micmash.

This noble son was willing to risk his life, trusting God, not men, for the victory. To his companion he suggested: "Come, let's go over to the outpost of those uncircumcised fellows. Perhaps the Lord will act on our behalf. Nothing can hinder the Lord from saving, whether by many or few" (I Samuel 14:6). What a contrast! Saul panicked over the dwindling numbers of his army. Jonathan found reason to trust in God even when the size of the enemy's army was overwhelming.

Would that we all had brothers in war like Jonathan's un-named armor-bearer! He responded to his commander's simple battle plan without hesitancy. "Do all that you have in mind . . . Go ahead; I am with you heart and soul" (I Samuel 14:7). Remember, as we pointed out in the last chapter, the only ones in the entire Israeli army with sword or spear in their possession were Saul and Jonathan.

Father and son both owned military weapons, but only Jonathan had the faith to use them when the odds were stacked against him. And the young armor-bearer at his side was likely headed into battle with just an ox-goad or a mattock!

Jonathan sought a clear indication of Yaweh's favor. He told his companion: "Come, then; we will cross over toward the men and let them see us. If they say to us, 'Wait there until we come to you,' we will stay where we are and not go up to them. But if they say, 'Come up to us,' we will climb up, because that will be our sign that the Lord has given them into our hands" (I Samuel 14:8-10).

God gave the sign of approval sought by Jonathan, and the pair proceeded to scale the cliff at the pass and encounter the enemy. Though badly outnumbered, the two of them killed some twenty Philistine soldiers in the first stage of that attack. The rout was on! The earth then shook and the Lord sent a powerful panic into the enemy camp. Saul and the six-hundred men with him observed the tumult and soon joined the battle. One man's faith in God inspired the same in many others!

As you may remember, Saul had hastily bound his troops with a reckless oath. If they ate anything before the conflict ended they were under a curse! Unaware of his father's oath, Jonathan renewed his flagging energy with some honey he came across in the woods. He nearly paid for that meal with his life. Take note that it was not disobedience to the Law of God that indicted the prince, it was the impulsive ego-driven legalism of King Saul which condemned him. That situation illustrates the danger of giving the absolute authority of a sovereign to a flawed human being.

When told of Saul's oath, the wise young leader quickly recognized the king's folly. "My father has made trouble for the country. See how my eyes brightened when I tasted a little of this honey. How much better it would have been if the men had eaten today some of the plunder they took from their enemies. Would not the slaughter of the Philistines have been even greater?" (I Samuel 14:29-30). God's providential provision of energy for His army was superior to the incentive supplied by any carnal ego-driven proclamation.

Saul had been rashly worried about his own vengeance and glory. Jonathan was more concerned for the glory of God, the success of the army, and the good of the nation. The distinction between father and son was becoming increasingly apparent. The former was evolving into a fearful, insecure, and self-absorbed despot. The son was developing into a confident young prince whose faith in God would be his guiding light.

The next time we encounter Jonathan he's bonding with a kindred spirit. A young shepherd named David had just accomplished what would have been virtually impossible in the ability of his flesh. He had brought an experienced warrior twice his size crashing to the ground. Here was a man of faith even greater than Jonathan's!

The Philistine champion, Goliath, had challenged the army of Israel to send a soldier out to meet him on the field of battle one on one. As the king, who was a greatly skilled and experienced warrior and who stood head and shoulders above his fellow Israelites, Saul would seem to be the logical choice to fight Goliath. Why didn't he rise to the challenge? Even Jonathan, a leader of real faith, never stepped forward. We're not told why in either instance.

Whatever the case, in the aftermath of David's supernatural triumph, Jonathan was compellingly drawn to him. The price for his friendship with the courageous shepherd who would replace his father as king would be high. Yet Jonathan would willingly relinquish his royal rank for the riches of his friendship with David.

Similarly, the Apostle Paul, whose pre-Christ status was prestigious in the natural, was willing to surrender that rank to the claims of Jesus. Feel the passion of Paul's life-altering decision as he expresses it in Philippians 3:7-9. "But whatever was to my profit I now consider loss for the sake of Christ. What is more, I consider everything a loss compared to the surpassing greatness of knowing Christ Jesus my Lord, for whose sake I have lost all things. I consider them rubbish, that I may gain Christ and be found in him, not having a righteousness of my own that comes from the law, but that which is through faith in Christ—the righteousness that comes from God and is by faith."

Jonathan's sentiments must have been similar to Paul's. He surrendered his princely rights to the Lord's anointed king (David), just as Paul relinquished his religious prestige in order to become the servant of Christ. The powerful bond between Jonathan and David was to become one of the most celebrated relationships in the Bible. It's a type of what our relationship with Christ Jesus should be. We have much to learn from it, but an extensive assessment of this bond must wait for a future chapter.

Through the years that would follow, Jonathan would manage to faithfully stand by his father whenever possible, while remaining loyal to his deep friendship with David. He occasionally faced his father's anger and rejection as a result of his steadfast allegiance to David. At one point Saul even attempted to kill Jonathan. Yet Israel's prince remained loyal to his father, fighting side by side against the enemies of Israel. In the end, this loving son and devoted servant of the Lord would valiantly fall on the same battlefield with his father and brothers.

Jonathan is a wonderful picture of the spiritual Christian . . . loving in all his relationships, yet always true to the Lord. He never reneged on his loyalty to his backslidden father, he simply made it subservient to a higher allegiance to God's anointed one. After all, aren't life's greatest lessons about priorities . . . and particularly in terms of our relationships?

Jonathan allowed the Lord to establish his priorities. Unlike his father, Saul, he surrendered to the new nature rather than the old nature. Jonathan would be ruled by the Word of God and the Holy Spirit. Whatever the cost, his supreme desire was to please God, not his own or anyone else's carnal nature.

More of Jonathan's exceptional character will be viewed in Chapter 6, as we study the attributes of his relationship with David. Jonathan was not perfect, mind you, but he was a very godly man. There is much about his life to be emulated by those of us who aim to pursue the kind of rich relationship with God that was intended by the Creator from the very beginning. Jonathan was truly a noble son.

CHAPTER 5

A Man after God's Own Heart

Before he appears on the stage of history, his remarkable nature is previewed with this assessment: "the Lord has sought out a man after his own heart and appointed him leader of his people . . ." (I Samuel 13:14). The phrase "a man after his own heart" immediately communicates to us a sense of the unique affinity this leader would have with his God. But what specifically does it mean? The understanding we seek will be played out before us as we observe the life of one of Scripture's most revered characters: David, son of Jesse.

Three chapters after we read the brief divine preview of his character, we gain our earliest sighting of the man himself. Samuel had been mourning for some time over Yaweh's rejection of Saul as king. God shook Samuel out of his gloomy paralysis by in essence declaring, "Enough is enough! It's time to move on!" God sent His servant to the home of Jesse of Bethlehem to anoint one of his sons as the new king over His people.

It's interesting to note that Samuel feared Saul would kill him once he heard about it. This tells us two things.

In spite of his great faith, the prophet was still human and susceptible to the negative emotion of fear. His concern also reveals that Samuel was aware of the emerging potent influence of the dark side of Saul. God stooped to Samuel's weakness and offered him a cover for his primary purpose in Bethlehem. "Take a heifer with you and say, 'I have come to sacrifice to the Lord'" (I Samuel 16:2).

Upon the arrival of Jesse and his sons for the sacrifice and ensuing feast, the search for the man after God's own heart began. The firstborn, Eliab, was presented to Samuel. He was quite impressed with Jesse's eldest, and his initial thoughts demonstrate that even spiritual leaders can miss the mark. The Lord's reaction to Samuel's misguided evaluation is illuminating. "Do not consider his appearance or his height, for I have rejected him. The Lord does not look at the things man looks at. Man looks at the outward appearance, but the Lord looks at the heart" (I Samuel 16:7).

The quest continued as one by one God passed on what appeared to be every last son of Jesse. Perhaps puzzled by this time, Samuel queried: "Are these all the sons you have?" (I Samuel 16:11). Jesse confessed that the baby of the family had been missing. He was out tending sheep. Was it the urgency of his shepherding responsibilities, or his father's negligible appraisal of him that accounted for his absence? We're not told.

The sacrificial feast was postponed as they waited for the lad. His arrival stirred the Spirit of the Lord within the elderly prophet, and as he had so many times before over the years, Samuel clearly heard Yaweh's voice. "Rise and anoint him; he is the one" (I Samuel 16:12). David was anointed in the presence of his brothers and the Spirit of God came upon him in power. Still, many years would pass before he would rightfully claim the crown that was his by divine plan.

While the spiritual authority to rule Israel now fell upon David, it had departed from Saul. Further, an evil (or injurious) spirit, authorized by the Almighty Himself, came to torment the rejected ruler (I Samuel 16:14). Scripture doesn't specify exactly what this troubling spirit was. It may have been demonic oppression, or it may have simply been a bad disposition, temper, or mood, The Hebrew word for spirit ("ruah") can support either interpretation.

It may be disturbing to envision God taking a hand in the sanctioning of such a harmful influence, but we must remember that human decisions have consequences. The Creator has established the rules of life and communicated them to us. Saul was merely reaping what he had sown. The Apostle Paul reminds us of this principle in Galatians 6:7,8. "Do not be deceived: God cannot be mocked. A man reaps what he sows. The one who sows to please his sinful nature, from that nature will reap destruction; the one who sows to please the Spirit, from the Spirit will reap eternal life."

The apostle's application of this principle in the case of a rebellious believer in the Corinthian church shows that God's purpose in dealing with His children in these matters is always redemptive. He tells the other members there to ". . . hand this man over to Satan, so that the sinful nature may be destroyed *and his spirit saved* on the day of the Lord" (I Corinthians 5:5).

It was more than coincidence that when Saul's attendants began a quest for someone to play the harp and soothe the king's troubled mind, they were led to

David. Besides trumpeting his skill as a musician, the servant who recommended him described him as ". . . a brave man and a warrior. He speaks well and is a fine-looking man. *And the Lord is with him*" (I Samuel 16:18).

When David played his harp Saul would find relief, and the evil spirit would leave. No wonder the king at first liked him. The powerful Spirit of God with David drove the tormenting presence from Saul every time his mind came under attack! The man after God's own heart ministered to the backslidden king whose disobedience had caused his own anointing from the Lord to depart.

In considering David's early vocation as a shepherd we gain the first inkling of how his heart reflected that of his God. The metaphor of the Lord as a shepherd and His people as sheep occurs throughout the Old Testament. David's own beloved twenty-third Psalm begins with the affirmation: "The Lord is my shepherd." In the New Testament, as the "image of the invisible God" (Colossians 1:15), Jesus identifies Himself as "the Good Shepherd" (John 10:11).

As a good shepherd himself, David understood the heart of God toward those under His care. Twice the young man had risked death to save his sheep. Like Yaweh, he was willing to lay down his life for the benefit of the flock. In II Samuel 5:12 we see this loving leadership style transferred from his responsibilities as shepherd in earlier years, to his duties in later years as king. David realized that his ascension to the throne was not simply for his own personal advantage. "And David knew that the Lord had established him as king over Israel and had exalted his kingdom *for the sake of his people Israel.*"

The most well known Bible story of all time about David reveals another vital aspect of his amazing connection with his Lord. Most of us heard the tale of David and Goliath when we were but children. We can likely recount it from memory. Let's take another look at it now with the aim of discovering more about this special man's heart after God.

Once more the enemy Philistines had gathered to make war upon God's people. But there was something unique about the situation this time. For forty days a single incredibly intimidating enemy warrior, who stood over nine feet tall, had dared the Israeli army to send their finest soldier to meet him in battle. The outcome of the struggle between the two would determine which people would become slaves to the other. As we pointed out in the last chapter, no one stepped forward to meet Goliath's challenge . . . not even Saul or Jonathan!

David's three older brothers were on the scene, serving with the army of Israel. Meanwhile David had been jockeying back and forth between tending his father's sheep and serving as Saul's minstrel. Jesse called his youngest son in from the pastures during one of those shepherding sessions, to run an errand to the battle front. David was to carry food provisions to his brothers and their unit commander, then report back to Jesse on the condition of his brothers.

David arrived just as the opposing armies were drawing up their lines. The Israelites were shouting their war cry. In the absence of an accompanying faith in God, however, their roar was hollow. When Goliath again shouted his defiance of Yaweh and His army, as he had for the previous forty days, the soldiers' bluster collapsed. Even the most hardened troops ran from the giant in terror.

The young man after God's own heart had a very different reaction. David was jealous for the Lord's honor, and saw this situation as a disgrace to Israel and their God. Like Aaron's grandson of old, Phinehas (Numbers 25:10,11), he had a great zeal for God's reputation. Upon hearing of the king's plea for a soldier to face Goliath in battle, and the reward offered the man who would respond, great faith rose within David.

Eliab, the eldest brother, overheard his kid brother's discussions with some of the Israeli soldiers on the matter, and burned with anger. Eliab presumed to do what only God can do: to know what is in the heart of a man (Jeremiah 17:9,10). "Why have you come down here? And with whom did you leave those few sheep in the desert? I know how conceited you are and how wicked your heart is; you came down only to watch the battle" (I Samuel 17:28).

David brushed aside his brother's judgmental rebuke and rejection, and pressed forward in faith. Eventually, the shepherd boy's words of confidence reached the ears of Saul, and the king sent for him. David proposed to fight the Philistine champion himself. Saul was skeptical in the beginning, calling attention to the vast difference in age, size, and military experience between the pair. David, however, related his experiences of killing a lion and a bear to protect his flock, and asserted that the same God who had given him victory over those fierce animals would deliver him from the hand of Goliath. One man viewed the crisis with the eyes of the flesh, while the other saw it through the eyes of faith.

In the course of making his argument for facing and defeating the massive warrior, David hit upon one of the key perspectives that set him apart from those who cowered before the enemy. He expected Goliath to fall just as the lion and bear had. ". . . this uncircumcised Philistine will be like one of them, *because he has defied the armies of the living God"* (I Samuel 17:36). David saw all of life as a war between good and evil, God and Satan, and he was ever standing up in faith for the honor of Yaweh!

In the face of the shepherd boy's unwavering trust in God, Saul relented, saying: "Go, and the Lord be with you" (I Samuel 17:37). The King did, however, try to equip David with his own battle armor and sword. David attempted to comply, but found himself too uncomfortable with the oversized and unfamiliar gear, and removed it. He then took his customary shepherd's staff, sling, and bag, and after carefully choosing five smooth stones, headed off to fight the giant.

David may have found comfort in his familiar weapons, but his trust rested in the power of his God. His Philistine opponent was insulted as he realized he was facing a mere boy. Goliath cursed David by his heathen gods and proclaimed that he would feed his flesh to the birds and beasts! David was unshaken.

"You come against me with sword and spear and javelin, but I come against you in the name of the Lord Almighty, the God of the armies of Israel, whom you have defied. This day the Lord will hand you over to me, and I'll strike you down and cut off your head. Today I will give the carcasses of the Philistine army to the birds of the air and the beasts of the earth, and the whole world will know that there is a God in Israel. All those gathered here will know that it is not by sword or spear that the Lord saves; for the battle is the Lord's, and he will give all of you into our hands" (I Samuel 17:45-47).

47

The stone in David's sling found its mark in the forehead of Goliath and he crashed facedown to the ground. The youthful warrior killed the enemy's champion and the Philistine soldiers fled the frontline in shock! Buoyed by David's astonishing victory, the men of Israel hurried after the Philistines and pursued them to the very gates of two of their chief stronghold cities. The way was littered with dead enemies, and the Israeli army subsequently plundered the abandoned Philistine camp.

In the wake of the battle, Saul and Abner, commander-in-chief of the army, inexplicably seemed not to know David. As David had been marching toward Goliath, the king asked Abner who the lad was. The commander didn't have the answer, and Saul ordered him to find out. Hadn't David been ministering in music to the tormented ruler? Wouldn't the head of the military also have met him at some point? Perhaps Abner had never encountered the shepherd/harpist during those dark hours of the king's tormenting oppression. Still, how could Saul forget his ministering angel so-to-speak?

We can only speculate as to Saul's problem remembering David. One or more of three factors may have contributed to his quandary. 1) David did not stay in the royal court continually (I Samuel 17:15) so the king may not have been as familiar with him as we might expect. 2) Saul may have been unable to reconcile David's previous musician identity with his present warrior persona. 3) Given Saul's erratic state of mind and the troublesome evil spirit which plagued him, his memory might easily have been affected.

Whatever the case, following David's return from slaying the giant, Abner sought him out, determined his origins, and brought him before Saul. As he spoke with David, the king became impressed by this young man. Someone else observing that same conversation, though, was *more* than impressed. Scripture tells us that ". . . Jonathan became one in spirit with David, and he loved him as he loved himself" (I Samuel 18:1). That spontaneous spiritual bonding quickly led to a covenant between them, one which will teach us much about our relationship with Christ. We'll discuss that covenant in some detail in the next chapter.

While Jonathan's friendship with David would endure, his father's fondness for the shepherd boy would swiftly disappear downstream with the turbulent rapids of a compromised life. In fact, that affection would turn to anger, jealousy and fear. The women of Israel greeted their homecoming heroes with music and dance. "As they danced they sang: 'Saul has slain his thousands, and David his tens of thousands'" (I Samuel 18:7). The divinely rejected leader, riddled with insecurity, was galled! The seeds of murder were planted in his heart.

The very next day, while Goliath's conqueror was playing his harp for Saul, the king was overcome by an evil spirit and hurled his spear at David. The young minstrel eluded him not once, but twice. In fear, because he knew the Lord was with David while He had departed from himself, Saul sent his perceived rival away and gave him command over a thousand troops. David's ensuing military successes and popularity with the people only increased as a result.

For a while the king plotted surreptitiously to end his competitor's life. Saul attempted to give his eldest daughter, Merab, to David in marriage, thinking the Philistines would more likely target him for death if he were the king's son-in-law. That proved unsuccessful as David humbly declined, asserting: "Who am I, and what is my family or my father's clan in Israel, that I should become the king's son-in-law?" (I Samuel 18:18).

Later, Saul offered David his younger daughter, Michal, who was deeply in love with David. Once more David demurred. This time, however, the king challenged his esteemed young commander to *earn* the right to marry into royalty by accomplishing success in a uniquely dangerous assignment against the enemy. Saul had hoped that this task would lead to David's demise at the hands of the Philistines. But again, empowered by the Spirit of God, David more than rose to the occasion. Following this victory the marriage went forward.

Saul continued his campaign to eliminate David through various means, even trying to enlist his own son, Jonathan, among others, to kill him. Every effort failed. Ultimately David had to flee from the king, pursued ruthlessly for years by the jealous sovereign. A small army of men were drawn to him during his fugitive wanderings. Through all this, the man after God's own heart refused to raise a weapon against Saul. Even when circumstances delivered the wayward king into his hands, David spared his life and addressed Saul with respect.

When Saul and Jonathan died together in their final battle, David mourned not only for his blood brother, Jonathan, but for Saul as well. Like the Lord Himself, David took no pleasure in the death of the one who resisted his divinely assigned authority. Ezekiel 33:11 reveals God's ideal desire for those who rebel against His righteous administration. There He proclaimed to His prophet: "As surely as I live, declares the Sovereign Lord, I take no pleasure in the death of the wicked, but rather that they turn from their ways and live."

Following Saul's death, an Amalekite came to David and claimed that he had ended the life of Saul. He expected to be rewarded for eliminating David's persecutor. Instead, the fugitive from years of Saul's murderous pursuit executed that Amalekite as an insolent assassin. He saw through the man's ruse. The Amalekite may have bowed before David and presented him with the crown, but his honor toward David was feigned. In his heart he remained the enemy of God's people. There's a spiritual parallel to this story. The flesh nature might be willing to go through the motions of honoring God in an attempt to gain favor, but will never truly submit to the sovereignty of Christ.

A long time would pass after Saul's death before God's anointed-in-waiting finally became ruler over the whole nation. David soon was made king over his own tribe of Judah, but a surviving son of Saul was crowned king over the remaining tribes. David waited seven years before he was able to ascend to his rightful throne over *all* of Israel. The man after God's own heart was nothing if not patient.

David was not sinless as was our Savior, but he is very much a type of Christ in this context. His original anointing by Samuel as leader of God's people is the most celebrated such event in the entire Old Testament. The Messiah (literally meaning "anointed one") descended from him and is referred to in Scripture as "the son of David." David lived his life (with a few notable exceptions) in faith and obedience to God, just as Christ would. And like Jesus, David refused to defend himself, leaving that to God.

As we examine David and Jonathan's friendship more closely in the next chapter, we'll come to see additional parallels between David and Jesus. Even more importantly, we'll gain a greater understanding of God's design for our special relationship with him through Christ Jesus.

CHAPTER 6

The Knitting Together
of Two Souls

Human friendship is a precious gift. Friendship with God is a gift whose worth is beyond description. David and Jonathan's relationship is to be celebrated as both. It's literally a true human friendship, and figuratively a wonderful divine/human one. As the latter, it teaches us symbolically much about what our relationship with the Lord is meant to be.

The bond between these two began with Jonathan's scrutiny of David during his post-Goliath conversation with King Saul. As Jonathan gazed and listened, his heart was roused as never before. David possessed in near fullness something Jonathan had owned in lesser measure. A unity of spirit between them was forged in love.

There is a natural attraction between kindred spirits. Common values encourage intense relationships. Such was the case with David and Jonathan. Jonathan loved David and David loved Jonathan. Love is Who God is (I John 4:16), and love is meant to be the foundation of all godly relationships.

That this pair were kindred spirits is undeniable. They shared common noble traits. They were both courageous warriors. Each had operated in faith, trusting the Lord for victory. David and Jonathan were men of godly humility, not dominated by carnal ambitions. They respected God-ordained leadership; David refusing to harm the backslidden King Saul, and Jonathan acknowledging David's royal calling.

Yet there was no question that David was the greater of the two. No one else in Israel but David had the faith to face the terrifying Goliath in combat . . . not even the valiant Jonathan. David had been anointed by God for the throne, Jonathan had not. Jonathan was heir to the fleshly dynasty of Saul, while David's leadership vocation had been born in the heart of God. Jonathan was a *descendent* of the *first Adam*, David the *forbearer* of the *last Adam: Jesus*. As was the case in the friendship between David and Jonathan, so it is with our relationship with Christ: the lesser partner is particularly drawn to the greater one.

That's the dynamic we see at work in the opening verses of I Samuel chapter 18. Allow me to again quote the latter half of the first verse. ". . . Jonathan became one in spirit with David, and he loved him as he loved himself." Verses 3 and 4 provide a demonstration of just how much the noble prince loved David. "And Jonathan made a covenant with David because he loved him as himself. Jonathan took off the robe he was wearing and gave it to David, along with his tunic, and even his sword, his bow and his belt."

The giving of gifts was a common part of the ancient covenants between men (more about the importance of that covenant later). Usually both parties offered gifts. In this situation *all* of the gifts appear to be from Jonathan to David. In a very real sense, however, like his descendent the Messiah, David had already given the gift of salvation to Jonathan and the whole nation through his victory over the enemy no one else could defeat.

The gifts Jonathan shared had unique significance. The Hebrew word simply translated "robe" in verse 4 is often used to indicate a *royal* robe. The implication was that the bestowing of this robe was a recognition by Jonathan that David was the rightful heir to the throne, even though as the eldest son of King Saul, Jonathan would likely have inherited the position himself upon his father's death. The gifts of his tunic, sword, bow, and belt would also suggest the prince's surrendering of his future throne to David.

Jonathan's words in I Samuel 23:17, spoken to encourage David while he was on the run from a murderous King Saul, seal the deal. "'Don't be afraid,' he said. 'My father Saul will not lay a hand on you. You will be king over Israel, and I will be second to you. Even my father Saul knows this.'" Jonathan was renouncing his claim to the crown in favor of God's chosen vessel. This is very much a picture of what is required of a true friend and disciple of Christ . . . total surrender of our rights to Jesus as Sovereign!

How different was Jonathan's attitude toward David's right to kingship than his father's. Both acknowledged David's ultimate ascension to the throne. But only Jonathan would relinquish his own claim to the crown in the process. Saul did admit David would one day be king (I Samuel 24:20), but not while Saul was living! Despite the fact that the Lord had rejected him as king, Saul refused to step down and let David take his God-ordained throne over Israel. Such an approach mirrors that of the carnal believer toward Christ. He may call Jesus King, but he never gives Him full authority in his own life.

This was not the first time in history that a man had rebelled against the Lord's sovereignty. Adam was given dominion over the earth, under the authority of the Creator. That glorious reign didn't last long. In the original sin of mankind he made a power grab, seeking to become his own God. The failed coup resulted in the entire globe being brought under the dominion of the Devil. As a consequence, we're all born sinners, living on a sinful planet and serving a sinful ruler: Satan.

Saul's sad story parallels that of Adam in several ways. Like Adam, Saul had authority from God bestowed on him. Just as Adam rejected the Word of the Lord, disobeyed, and subsequently lost his authority, so did Saul. Adam was more concerned with the shame of his nakedness than how his sin had disappointed his Creator. Saul cared more about the personal humiliation of his rejection as king than that his disobedience had offended God. Moreover, as Adam's tasting of the forbidden fruit resulted in experiencing the consequences of a firsthand knowledge of evil, so Saul's rebellion opened the door for his encounters with an evil spirit.

The *first* Adam had been sinless for a time, but only because he was created in innocence. When faced with temptation he failed the test through unbelief and disobedience. The *last* Adam, Jesus (I Corinthians 15:45), was conceived in innocence too, but remained sinless in the face of temptation by always acting in faith and obedience. Without fear of contradiction Jesus was able to declare ". . . I do nothing on my own but speak just what the Father has taught me. The one who sent me is with me; he has not left me alone, for I always do what pleases him" (John 8:28,29).

In operating entirely under the lawful rule of God, the *last* Adam set the stage for the restoration of the Creator's image and authority in those who become Jesus' blood brothers. That's why Romans 8:29 can declare that those who are born again and love God are destined ". . . to be conformed to the likeness of his Son, that he might be the firstborn among many brothers."

Just as Jonathan expected to reign with David when the "man after God's own heart" ascended to the throne, so we who acknowledge Jesus' right to govern in our hearts can anticipate someday ruling under him. The Apostle Paul affirms this in II Timothy 2:11,12: "Here is a trustworthy saying: If we died with him, we will also live with him; if we endure, we will also reign with him." In Revelation 5:10 the angel says of those who have been redeemed by the blood of Christ: "You have made them to be a kingdom and priests to serve our God, and they will reign on the earth."

The path to the fulfillment of such a marvelous divine destiny, however, begins with our stepping down from the throne of our lives and submitting to the legitimate absolute authority of Christ. Jesus must be not only our Savior, but our Lord and Master as well. He alone is entitled to wear the crown. It required great trust for Jonathan to covenant with a man who would take the throne that would have been his by natural succession. That kind of submission involves deep conviction. So does our surrender to Jesus.

As he did with Adam and Eve, Satan will whisper into our ears that real happiness lays in being our own god. The devil sows distrust and disobedience toward the Lord. He's promoting a hoax. if we follow his perverse advice we don't really end up in charge anyway. In attempting to retain the throne, we soon discover that we're actually slaves to an evil tyrant. The enemy of our souls rules over our hearts through the carnal nature within us, created in the image of the ultimate rebel: Satan. We end up exchanging the loving administration of God for the hateful tyranny of the devil!

While David's rising national popularity and God-ordained empowerment led to rising vitriol from Saul, Jonathan remained faithful to his friend. The godly prince risked rejection by his father and even death at the hand of Saul (see I Samuel 20:30-33) to stand by his fugitive covenant companion. Real godly friendship is a matter of enduring commitment, even when that commitment spells trouble for one or both parties. It's based upon unselfish love.

Scripture cites three times when Jonathan came to David's aid in what were dire circumstances for the latter. During the second of those occasions the two of them renewed their original covenant, extending it to include their respective families (I Samuel 20:16,17). As we'll discuss later, this enlarged covenant tent would be critical for one family member in particular.

In this same narrative we see another demonstration of Jonathan's intense dedication to his friend. After David asserted that he was certain there was only one step between him and the execution of a death warrant from Saul, Jonathan offered *unconditional* support. "Whatever you want me to do, I'll do for you" (I Samuel 20:4). This is the same level of commitment every true child of God ought to give to Christ. Lord, help us to follow Jonathan's example!

Let's take some time now to examine the special covenant between these men more closely. Covenants were originally initiated by God. The very first one is revealed in Genesis chapter 6, where the Lord made a covenant with Noah and his family. There are numerous covenants mentioned in the Bible. Some were between God and humans and others only between people. However, covenants are not limited to the Scripture. They have been part of earthly cultures since ancient times.

In an effort to explain what covenants are, allow me to quote from a pertinent passage in my earlier book, **The Curse**:

> "Covenant as presented in Scripture is not a concept readily familiar to moderns. The English word 'covenant' does not convey the full sense of a Biblical covenant. Other similar terms such as alliance, agreement, contract, pact, and treaty, also fall far short. The Hebrew word translated 'covenant' throughout the Old Testament does lay a foundation for our understanding. It comes from a root word meaning 'to fetter.' Clearly a covenant 'fetters' or bonds two parties together. But the nature and manner of that bonding in a Biblical covenant is unique . . . so unique that there is no single word or concept in English adequate to communicate it . . .

A Biblical covenant is a formal bonding of two or more parties, powerfully obligating one or more of them to certain stipulations. That commitment was so solemn that to break it would be considered high treason, generating dire consequences for such a breach. The sacrificial death of an animal at the sealing of the covenant, signified the solemnity of the relationship. The shedding of life blood was central to the covenant."

There were often other traditions associated with covenant making, such as the aforementioned giving of gifts, and often the sharing of a meal. But the critical role of the shedding of blood in covenant making is why this book is titled **Blood Brothers**. That's what Jonathan and David became when they covenanted. In II Samuel 1:26, while mourning Jonathan's death, David declared: "I grieve for you, Jonathan *my brother.*" Their covenant bond was as strong as any familial bond could ever be!

In further clarifying the central place of blood in Biblical covenant, we should note that the Hebrew word translated "made" in the phrase "made a covenant," literally means "to cut." In other words they "*cut* a covenant." Though only implied in this phrase, and the narrative doesn't specifically mention it, the inclusion of the shedding of blood was so fundamental to covenants that it goes without saying. We'll discover just how vital life blood is to a relationship with God in our final chapter.

David and Jonathan's covenant love for each other would have to withstand much strain. Repeatedly Jonathan exposed his father's plots to take his blood brother's life, sometimes risking his own life in the process. Did they enjoy good times together? Though there is no direct mention of these type of events in the Biblical account, I'm confident they shared pleasurable meals, celebrations, and possibly even recreational activities. Still, loving relationships do not guarantee an unbroken string of joyous fellowship, and David's and Jonathan's friendship was no exception.

Despite the difficulties, this special relationship would endure. True friendship is not lost in hard times. Adversity deepens brotherhood. As previously mentioned, the pair even renewed their covenant in the midst of intense troubles (I Samuel 23:18). Jonathan's devoted friendship was of great encouragement to David during his years on the run. In I Samuel 23:16 we're provided a clear example. "And Saul's son Jonathan went to David at Horesh and helped him find strength in God." In his humanity, even Christ sometimes sought to draw strength from His Heavenly Father through His earthly friends. In His time of deepest distress He asked His disciples to "stay here and keep watch" (Mark 14:34).

At one of David's and Jonathan's clandestine meetings we witness a touching scene of brotherly affection. Jonathan had once more protected David by alerting him to yet another murderous plot. Scripture notes that before they parted David ". . . bowed down before Jonathan three times, with his face to the ground. Then they kissed each other and wept together – but David wept the most" (I Samuel 20:41).

When informed of his blood brother's death in battle on Mount Gilboa, David wrote and recited a moving eulogy, memorializing Jonathan's gracious and courageous spirit, and his wonderful love for his covenant friend. In that remarkable piece of prose David even celebrated the successes of the man who had ruthlessly sought to destroy him: King Saul. Then he ordered his own men to memorize this heartfelt lament.

David's one-on-one covenant relationship with Jonathan had expired with the passing of the latter. But remember, that covenant had been extended to cover their families as well. Apparently years later this recollection stirred in David's heart. He had finally been established on the throne for which he had been anointed so long ago. Yet he had not forgotten the man whose friendship had been so precious. He sought an opportunity to reach out to Jonathan's family. "David asked, 'Is there anyone still left of the house of Saul to whom I can show kindness for Jonathan's sake?'" (II Samuel 9:1).

The research that followed the king's inquiry yielded a story of misfortune. One of Jonathan's sons was alive, but lived as a cripple in Lo Debar. His tragic tale had been briefly cited earlier, in II Samuel 4:4. "Jonathan son of Saul had a son who was lame in both feet. He was five years old when the news about Saul and Jonathan came from Jezreel. His nurse picked him up and fled, but as she hurried to leave, he fell and became crippled. His name was Mephibosheth."

David had this son of his beloved blood brother brought to him immediately. Mephibosheth bowed before him to pay honor to the man whose reign had displaced that of his own family. The king quickly allayed any fears of retribution for the sins of his grandfather that Mephibosheth may have harbored. "'Don't be afraid,' David said to him, 'for I will surely show you kindness for the sake of your father

Jonathan. I will restore to you all the land that belonged to your grandfather Saul, and you will always eat at my table'" (II Samuel 9:7).

Wow! Perhaps that word is not appropriately majestic to describe this gracious act of Israel's sovereign, but it is an honest gut reaction. David's covenant love for Jonathan had been extended to the latter's surviving son without hesitation. He stood true to his commitment to show kindness to Jonathan's family.

In addition to restoring all of his grandfather's property to Mephibosheth, David established a caretaker for that land so that Mephibosheth would not have to worry about the day to day operations of the farm. Jonathan's offspring became like one of the king's own sons. The final verse of II Samuel chapter 9 creates a charming image of this tender relationship. "And Mephibosheth lived in Jerusalem, because he always ate at the king's table, and he was crippled in both feet."

At this point the parallels between David and Jesus Christ, the Son of God, cry out for recognition. The Lord's covenant with His people had always reached to their descendents. It began with the promise He made to Abraham in Genesis 17:7. "I will establish my covenant as an everlasting covenant between me and you and your descendants after you for the generations to come, to be your God and the God of your descendants after you." Subsequently, we see the umbrella of God's covenant with Abraham, covering *all* Israel, reiterated numerous times throughout the Old Testament.

In the New Testament we find that the Messianic (or New) Covenant also reaches beyond first generation believers. When an astounded jailer in Philippi witnessed

God's supernatural intervention on behalf of His servants Paul and Silas, he urgently asked how he too, could be saved. "Believe in the Lord Jesus, and you will be saved—you and your household" (Acts 16:31). While I don't believe this promise nullifies the free will of the family members of Christians, I am convinced it indicates God's relentless efforts to bring them to the place of surrender to His marvelous salvation in Christ.

Dear child of God, I want you to envision Jesus standing this day as the Great Intercessor at the right hand of God the Father in Heaven. Then hear Him as He asks much like David of old, "Is there anyone of my blood brother's family to whom I can show kindness for their sake?"

Mephibosheth had lived in Lo Debar, which means "without pasture." Such is the condition of our unsaved relatives. They're outside the lush pastures of the Good Shepherd. Just as Jesse's shepherd son sought an opportunity to provide for Jonathan's crippled lamb, so Jesus waits to lead your loved ones into His redemptive care. Believe me . . . no, believe the Word of God . . . He longs to bring your lost sheep under the security blanket of His fold. Crippled by sin though they may be, His grace and mercy reaches out to them!

Such are some of the blessings of those who peer intently into the eyes of David's Greater Son, Jesus of Nazareth. Our souls are knit together with His. So don't stop your pursuit. The rewards are too great to lose. "And we, who with unveiled faces all reflect [or contemplate] the Lord's glory, are being transformed into his likeness with ever-increasing glory, which comes from the Lord, who is the Spirit" (II Corinthians 3:18).

CHAPTER 7

The New Covenant

In 1989 I had the privilege of doing a radio interview with a great man of God whose ministry positively influenced my walk with the Lord. In the process of introducing Major W. Ian Thomas to my listeners, I mentioned the three books he had written and I had read. I inadvertently misspoke the title of one of those books. I referred to it as "The Saving *Grace* of Christ." Major Thomas kindly corrected me, saying that the title was actually "The Saving *Life* of Christ." He then pointed out how critical a difference the exchange of a single word could make in signifying the heart of his subject.

"Most folks, you see, think of His saving *death*," my guest explained. "That's gloriously true. Through that alone we have redemption. But the marvelous thing is that what He did when He died on the cross was to make it possible for Him to share his *life* with us on earth on the way to heaven. It's His life that saves us. His death makes it possible for Him to live His life in us and through us. And that's the Christian life."

Major Thomas was right. As Christians we tend to focus on the death of our Savior as an end in itself. As indispensable as that substitutionary death is, it's only the gateway to the New Covenant Jesus created for those who would put their faith in Him. Understand please, that the essence of covenant is the sharing of *life*. The death of Christ is the means of restoring our previously lost relationship with God. And through that restored relationship God shares His *life* with us.

In John 10:10,11 the words of Jesus mark the stark contrast between Him and the god of this present age, the Devil. "The thief comes only to steal and kill and destroy; I have come that they may have life, and have it to the full. I am the good shepherd. The good shepherd lays down his life for the sheep." Jesus endured the torturous Roman-designed form of execution called crucifixion so that we, His sheep, might possess life to the full measure.

When facing His death, Jesus plainly understood that it was essential to His mission. As the time of His cruel punishment for our sins approached, He acknowledged to his disciples: "Now my heart is troubled, and what shall I say? 'Father, save me from this hour?' No, it was for this very reason I came to this hour. Father, glorify your name!" (John 12:27,28). Christ had come to restore God's loving bond with mankind. "For God so loved the world that he gave his one and only Son, that whoever believes in him shall not perish but have eternal life. For God did not send his Son into the world to condemn the world, but to save the world through him" (John 3:16,17).

His death was the seed that would generate life. "I tell you the truth, unless a kernel of wheat falls to the ground and dies, it remains only a single seed. But if it dies it produces many seeds" (John 12:24). When Adam and Eve sinned, all humanity died with them to the richly fulfilling relationship the Creator had originally intended for us to enjoy with Him. Jesus death not only paid the penalty for our sin, it opened the door for a new life with God.

This *new* life springs into existence as we become a *new* creation (II Corinthians 5:17). The death of Christ is the emancipation proclamation from slavery to the old nature for all who believe in Him. Romans 6:6,7 alludes to that grand spiritual document. "For we know that our old self was crucified with him so that the body of sin might be done away with, that we should no longer be slaves to sin—because anyone who has died has been freed from sin."

Such freedom is *legally* ours when we become Christians, but it must be individually *appropriated* by faith. ". . . Count yourselves dead to sin but alive to God in Christ Jesus" (Romans 6:11). We see the Apostle Paul take his own personal stand of faith in this matter when he declares: "I have been crucified with Christ and I no longer live, but Christ lives in me. The life I live in the body, I live by faith in the Son of God, who loved me and gave himself for me" (Galatians 2:20). It's critical that we believe Jesus can live His life through us. We must walk by faith in the expectation that His indwelling presence empowers us to do what we cannot do in ourselves.

Yet even the great apostle had to admit that this freedom from the carnal man who has dominated us is a work in progress. "Not that I have already obtained all this, or have already been made perfect, but I press on to take hold of that for which Christ Jesus took hold of me. Brothers, I do not consider myself yet to have taken hold of it. But one thing I do: Forgetting what is behind and straining toward what is ahead, I press on toward the goal to win the prize for which God has called me heavenward in Christ Jesus. All of us who are mature should take such a view of things. And if on some point you think differently, that too God will make clear to you. Only let us live up to what we have already attained" (Philippians 3:12-16).

The liberty that's provided through our Savior's *death* must be exercised in the *life* that flows through His resurrection. Paul's personal hunger to know Jesus intimately has this as its glorious expectation. "I want to know Christ and the power of his resurrection and the fellowship of sharing in his sufferings, becoming like him in his death, and so, somehow, to attain to the resurrection from the dead" (Philippians 3:10,11).

The New Covenant we enter into with Jesus is foreshadowed in several ways by the ancient covenant between Jonathan and David. At their core both covenants were a sharing of life and love through a cherished brotherly relationship. Incredibly, God has ordained that those who come into the New Covenant should be considered Jesus' family. We're more than just disciples. We're blood relatives! "Both the one who makes men holy and those who are made holy are of the same family. So Jesus is not ashamed to call them brothers" (Hebrews 2:11).

Just as David and Jonathan became blood brothers through covenant, so do Jesus and we. Entering into the New Covenant with Jesus means sharing His life. His interests become our interests. His family becomes our family. His enemies become our enemies. All that is ours belongs to Him . . . and better yet, all that is His is ours!

As we said before, blood was a crucial element in covenant making. The provision of that blood normally required a sacrificial death . . . usually of an animal. For the New Covenant, that blood flowed in death from Christ, Who is in numerous places in Scripture referred to as "the Lamb of God."

We most naturally associate the shedding of blood primarily with death. It's critical, however, that we grasp that even more importantly, blood represents *life*! In Leviticus 17:11 the Lord establishes this understanding with His people. "For the life of a creature is in the blood, and I have given it to you to make atonement for yourselves on the altar; it is the blood that makes atonement for one's life." Through their blood covenant David and Jonathan shared *their lives*. And through the blood of Christ we share *His life*.

In the sacrament (or ordinance) of communion we celebrate the life that flows from His death. Communion is symbolic of the requisite spiritual transaction by which we enter into covenant with Christ. That's what Jesus unequivocally insisted upon in John 6:53. "I tell you the truth, unless you eat the flesh of the Son of Man and drink his blood, you have no life in you." Some of His disciples found this so difficult to accept that they no longer followed Him after that. *Life* as God the Father intended it to be is available only through the sacrificial body and blood of Christ.

Jonathan became one in spirit with David and loved him as himself. When we are born again we become one with Christ. His Spirit lives in us. We share His life. All that is His is available to us, and all that is ours should belong to Him. Ahhhhh . . . but that's often the sticking point when it comes to enjoying the fullness of the covenant. We hold back. Remember, faith and obedience are essential to our walk with the Lord. Do we really love the Lord Jesus? The test of our love is simple according to Him. In John 14:15 He says, "If you love me, you will obey what I command." The achievement of total obedience in our walk with the Lord is the major issue for most of us as believers.

Author and speaker Stuart Briscoe found it to be so. In the early years following his conversion he saw his relationship with Jesus as simply a ticket to *get out of hell.* He decided: "This is easy!" As time passed he came to see that God had a purpose for him in *this life.* Beginning to make the effort to live righteously, he determined: "It's difficult." But this ongoing endeavor produced frustration as he repeatedly fell far short of divine standards. In exasperation he sighed: "It's impossible!" That's when he began to understand that the only way to live the Christian life was to allow the indwelling Christ to do it through him.

This is the point each of us must reach. For as Jesus told His disciples in Mark 10:27: "With man this is impossible, but not with God: all things are possible with God." We must acknowledge the total bankruptcy of the carnal nature. It simply cannot live a life that's pleasing to the Lord. We must depend on our new nature: the presence of Christ within us. Just as the springboard to our salvation was faith in Jesus, so should that faith be the access to the power to live for Him. Like Paul in the previously mentioned passage from Galatians 2:20, we must declare: "The life I live in the body, I live by faith in the Son of God . . ."

Now let's ponder for a moment the compelling attraction Jonathan had to David, and the implications it carries for the magnetism of our Lord Jesus. The immediate context in the first few verses of I Samuel chapter 18 doesn't specifically reveal the reasons why Jonathan was so drawn to David. But by contemplating the larger surrounding picture we can gain some insight.

The young shepherd had just toppled the giant no one else in Israel had the courage to face. His faith in Yaweh was so strong that he had entered the combat with supreme confidence. Yet when King Saul asked who he was, David responded in humility: "I am the son of *your servant* Jesse of Bethlehem" (I Samuel 17:58). Other details of his conversation with Saul are not recorded. But we have enough information to begin to see why Jonathan was so immediately and powerfully taken with God's anointed vessel.

When we look to the life of Jesus the Messiah (Anointed One), we see that He not only shared David's admirable traits . . . He far exceeded them! Courage, faith, and humility are just the tip of the proverbial iceberg as we begin to examine the life of Christ. Traits such as love, knowledge, and authority must be quickly added to a list of virtues that is inexhaustible.

The effect is that His followers found His appeal irresistible. Fishermen, tax collectors, and even hardened skeptics left their former lives without hesitation, and faced risks, persecutions, and hardships to attach themselves to this Stranger of Galilee. They would give up whatever was necessary to enjoy His companionship. The result of their discipleship would, over the course of time and through divine endowment, be a marvelous transformation. These men would become like their Master. Others would later simply take note ". . . that these men had been with Jesus" (Acts 4:13).

How about us? Have we really seen Jesus? Are we enthralled with God's Anointed One? Have we become His blood brothers? Are we being conformed to His image? We tend to become like the people with whom we spend time. So we must spend time with our divine companion. We do that through daily devotions, remaining in a constant attitude of prayer, being sensitive to His voice throughout the day, allowing Him to carry out His mission to others through us, and gathering with fellow believers in His house.

Perhaps the most important question is: have we surrendered the throne of our heart to Him? Christ is our dear brother and friend, but above all else He is our King. There must be only one true sovereign in the universe . . . and only one true sovereign in our souls. Satan once tried to steal God's throne in the annals of eternity. Then using the first human beings as surrogates, again attempted to usurp the crown that is not his.

If we're to experience the wonderful life that the Lord designed for us, we must recognize God's prior claim to kingship and yield to it. Some see this divine demand as a form of despotism. They view the Lord as just another aspiring dictator, no better than any of the long procession of tyrants who have cruelly oppressed their fellowmen throughout history. In this perspective they fail to take into account two vital factors.

Number one, God *alone* has rightful claim to the crown. He designed and created all things in this universe, including our very lives. In Acts 17:26-28 Paul explained this to the Athenians. "From one man he made every nation of men, that they should inhabit the whole earth; and he determined the times set for them and the exact places where they should live. God did this so that men would seek him and perhaps reach out for him and find him, though he is not far from each one of us. 'For in him we live and move and have our being.' As some of your own poets have said, 'We are his offspring.'" No human leader on earth can make these assertions.

Secondly, *only* God has the ability to rule with uncorrupted character. Lord Acton, British historian, wrote: "Power tends to corrupt, and absolute power corrupts absolutely. Great men are almost always bad men." He was correct. Fallen man cannot endure the lures of absolute power. That God is able to rule perfectly is based primarily upon two of His attributes. The Apostle John tells us that "God is *Love*" (I John 4:8). This means His motives toward us are always pure. God is also *omniscient*, or all knowing. Consequently, He knows at all times what is happening in our lives and what is best for us.

Believing these truths enables us to confidently surrender to His sovereignty. The rewards of that decision are priceless both for now and eternity. In this life our total trust in and commitment to the Lord can provide divine peace in every circumstance. His companionship is more fulfilling than that of any other. And in the life to come we'll not only continue to enjoy that friendship, but also share His authority through our incorruptible new nature.

One of the most stirring pictures for me in all of the Bible is the scene in Revelation 19:11-16. There we see Jesus returning to earth to put an end to the evil reign of Satan through fallen man, and we are accompanying our Lord in this, His ultimate triumph. That will be a glorious moment of consummation for those who have surrendered to the sovereignty of Christ!

"I saw heaven standing open and there before me was a white horse, whose rider is called Faithful and True. With justice he judges and makes war. His eyes are like blazing fire, and on his head are many crowns. He has a name written on him that no one knows but he himself. He is dressed in a robe dipped in blood, and his name is the Word of God. The armies of heaven were following him, riding on white horses and dressed in fine linen, white and clean. Out of his mouth comes a sharp sword with which to strike down the nations. 'He will rule them with an iron scepter.' He treads the winepress of the fury of the wrath of God Almighty. On his robe and on his thigh he has this name written: king of kings and lord of lords."

Have you caught a glimpse of Jesus? Has a deep hunger stirred within you? If you haven't already done so, make the choice now to enter the fullness of the New Covenant with Him. Turn the throne of your life over to the rightful King and let Him live through you. Then gladly proclaim your Blood Brother as "King of *me* and Lord of *me*!"